This book belongs to:

Color With Me!

Mommy & Me Coloring Book

Spring & Summer

Sandy Mahony & Mary Lou Brown

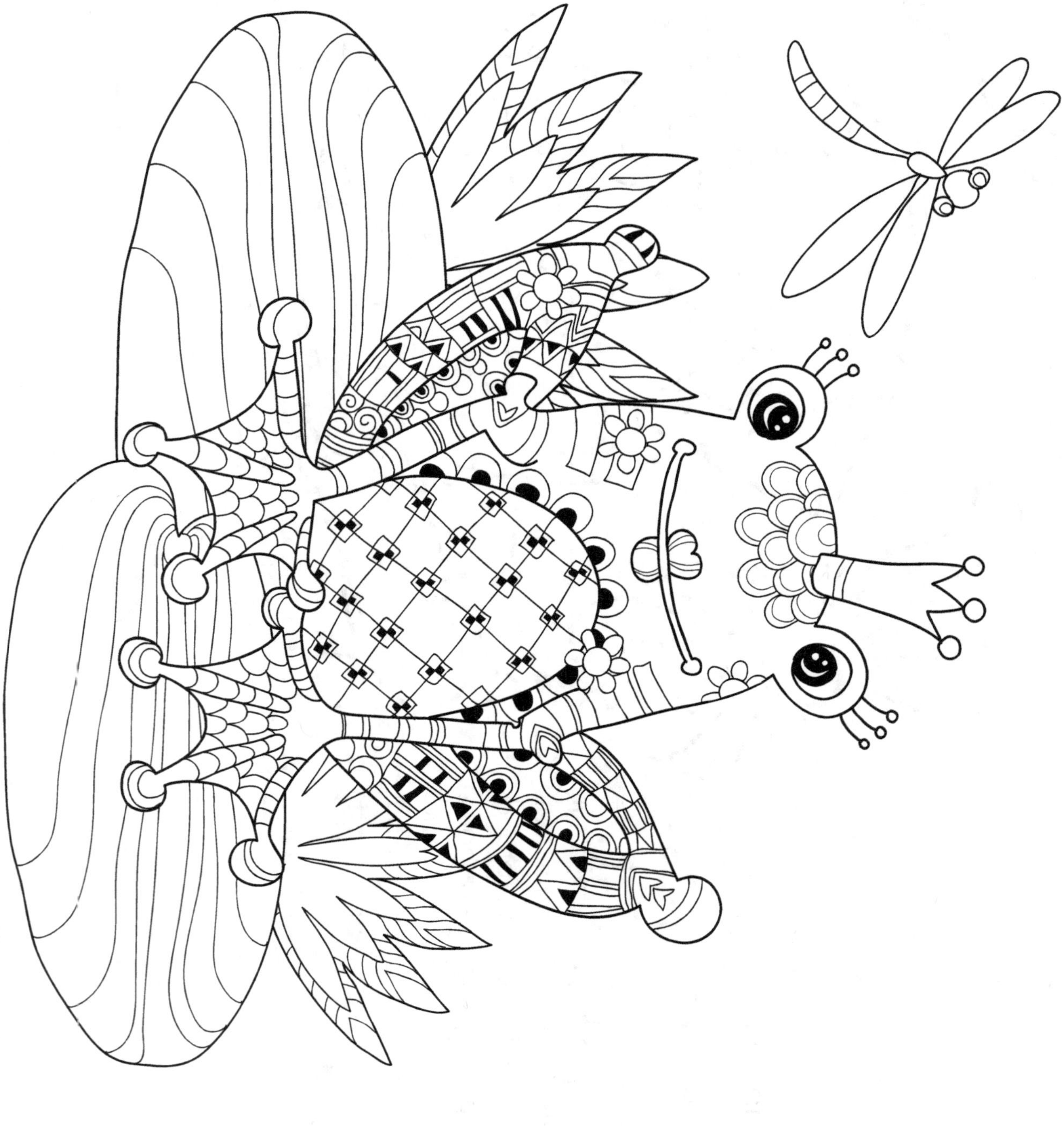

GARDEN

HAPPY MOTHER'S DAY!
HAPPY MOTHER'S DAY!

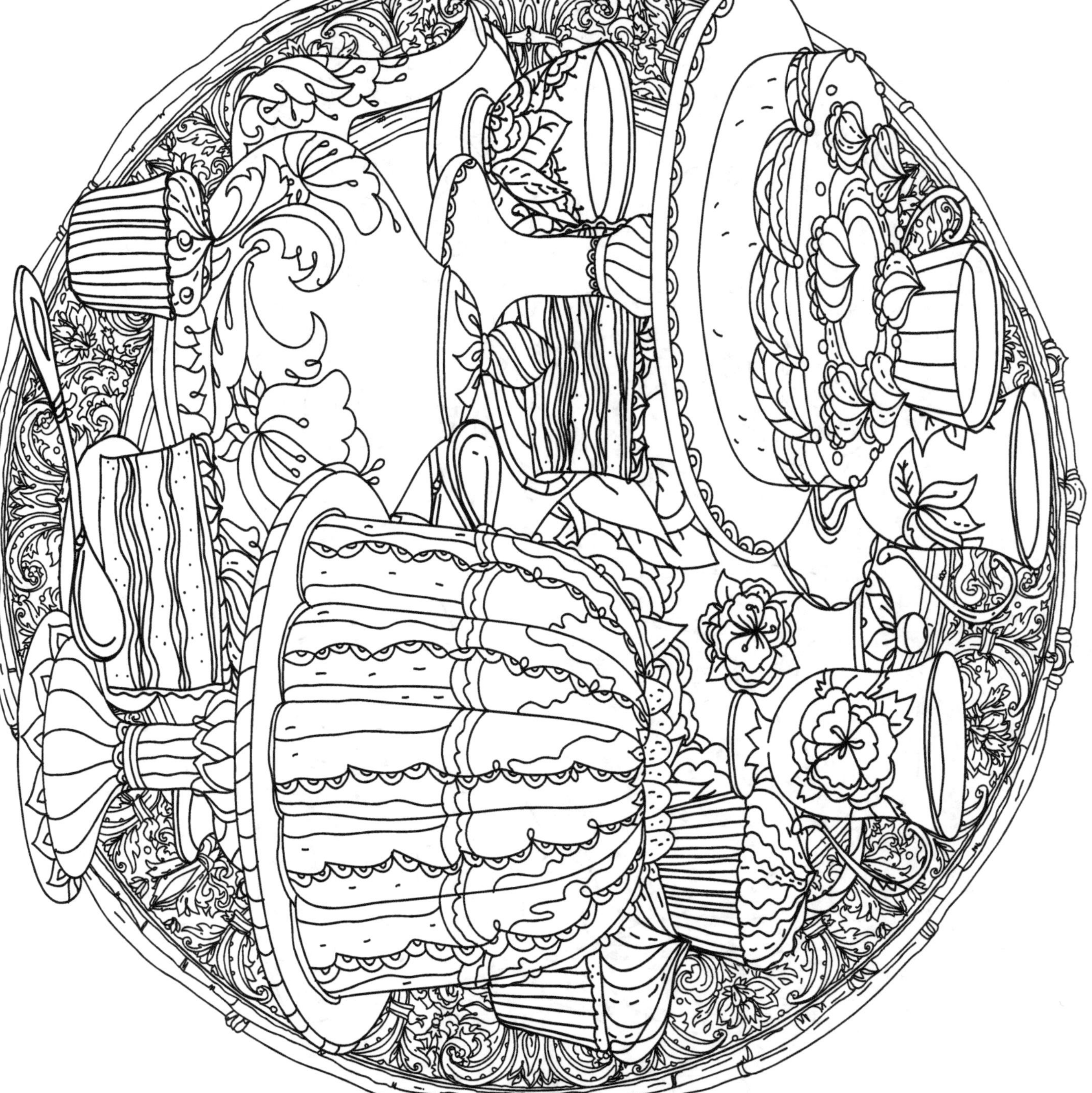

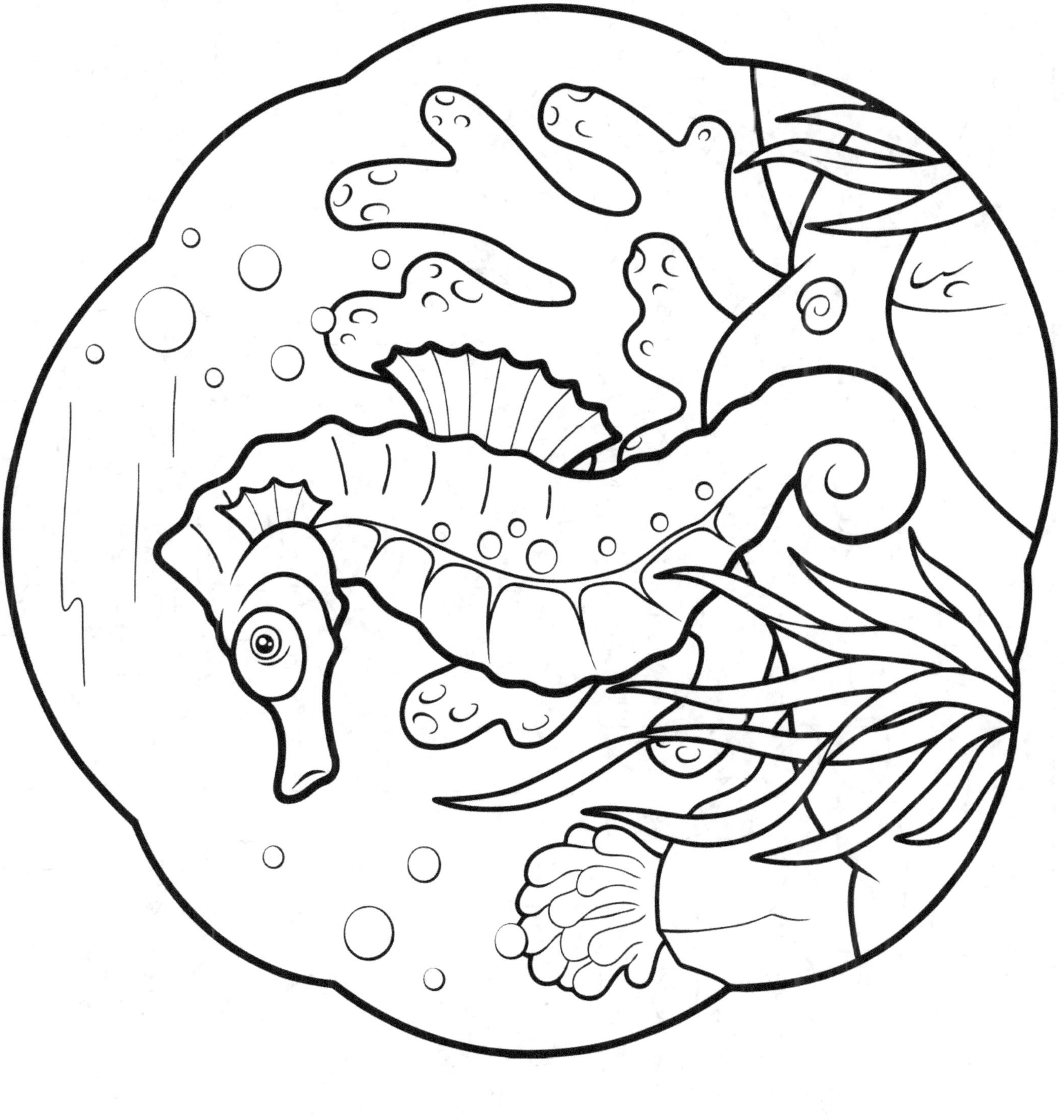

Adventure
Learning Press

www.ingramcontent.com/pod-product-compliance
Lightning Source LLC
Chambersburg PA
CBHW081542280526
45788CB00010B/3332
9781530079049